Eat to Run

Smoothies for Runners
Volume 1

32 Proven Smoothie Recipes to Take Your Running
Performance to the Next Level, Decrease Your
Recovery Time and Allow You to Run Injury-free

CJ Hitz

Eat to Run: Smoothies for Runners
Volume 1

Body and Soul Publishing

ISBN-13: 978-0615626239
ISBN-10: 0615626238

Printed in the United States of America

Order more copies at: www.SmoothiesforRunners.com

Table of Contents
Smoothies for Runners

Introduction

Smoothie. Doesn't that word just roll off the tongue nicely?

The smoothie has to be one of the greatest inventions (or accidents) in the world of food. But for the runner, it can be one of our best friends as we'll get into later.

Smoothies started appearing in the late 1960s when ice cream vendors and health food stores began selling them. By the 1990s, these blended creations could be found in cafes, coffee houses and health clubs as the health and nutrition industry took off.

Today, you'll find business chains dedicated to the smoothie like Starbucks is dedicated to coffee. Some of these include Smoothie King, Tropical Smoothie Café, The Smoothie Company and Jamba Juice. In the last ten years, we've also seen pre-bottled versions show up on supermarket shelves all over the world.

I've been a big fan of smoothies for years. Not only are there endless combinations that taste great, but these same combinations can do wonders for your health. Smoothie flavors are limited only by your imagination.

What Is A Smoothie?

Unfortunately, the term 'smoothie' has been a little watered down (no pun intended) through the years. Many a customer has bought what they thought was a smoothie when they were really sold a "healthy" milkshake.

Let's take a look at a couple different dictionary definitions...

smooth·ie – a thick beverage of fruit pureed in a blender with ice and milk, yogurt, or juice. (Random House Dictionary)

smooth·ie – a creamy beverage made of fruit blended with juice, milk, or yogurt. (Merriam-Webster)

The key ingredient for a smoothie in its simplest form should be fruit. Can a smoothie contain milk and yogurt? I believe they can but I would like to suggest alternatives in this book that would also be approved of in the vegan running community.

In every smoothie recipe found in this book, at least one fruit will be one of the ingredients. Some will have more. But in my humble opinion, when you remove fruit, you no longer have a smoothie on your hands. There have been times (and they are few) when I did not have fruit on hand. In these instances, I call it a "shake" which might include rice milk, protein powder, nuts and flax seeds as an example.

I look forward to exploring the world of smoothies with you as we seek to give our bodies what they truly crave both before and after a run.

To health!

Breaking Down Your Smoothie:

The Benefits of Specific Smoothie Ingredients For Runners

As a runner, you're constantly breaking down your body with each and every workout. There are training adaptations taking place that allow you to push to new levels as you build strength and endurance. Isn't it a wonderful feeling when you set that new personal best? Finishing your long run with less soreness and more energy is a sure sign that you're making progress. It's also very satisfying when you hit your goal pace in each of those 12x400m track repeats.

Consistency in training will take us a long way on the road to running success but it can only take us so far. I would argue that what we *feed* our bodies is just as important as the training itself. Inconsistency and compromise in our diet will yield mediocre results in our training adaptations. Simply put, you are what you eat.

Since the spring of 2008, I've learned some hard lessons when it comes to training and nutrition. I've learned what my body can endure and when I've crossed into overtraining. Listening to your body is crucial as you move forward as a runner. Part of that listening includes knowing what our bodies are crying out for in the area of nutrients. What does the human body require in order to function most efficiently?

The fact that you bought this book is proof that you care about what you put into your own body. Feeding your body a steady diet of junk food will lead to injury and burnout over the course of time. Feeding your body a healthy smoothie will not only give you cleaner fuel and better building blocks for recovery, but you'll also notice your body thanking you as you satisfy it with what it truly craves.

This section isn't meant to be exhaustive but I'd like to mention some benefits for runners found in the key ingredients listed in the smoothie recipes I share. Though each recipe is different, you'll notice many of these powerful ingredients showing up in many of the smoothies listed. You could call them smoothie staples.

There should be purpose in each smoothie we blend. Randomly throwing things into your blender without really thinking can be a waste...both for your body and your bank account.

Let's take a deeper look at why some of these ingredients will become recurring themes in the smoothies ahead...

Nature's Anti-Inflammatories

If you've been running long enough you've probably reached for the bottle of Ibuprofen. This has been a common practice for many runners, especially those who train for marathons and ultras regularly. The primary reason has been to decrease inflammation which is where our soreness comes from after breaking down muscle tissue.

Unfortunately, there are multiple long-term consequences linked to this "wonder" pill. Some of these include gastrointestinal ulcers and bleeding, damage to tissues of the rectum and kidney damage. Erik Skaggs, a talented trail runner, suffered renal failure and kidney problems as a result of his overuse of Ibuprofen during the 2009 Where's Waldo 100k.

Dark, colorful berries are a much healthier alternative to help with running inflammation. Wild blueberries score near the top in terms of the antioxidants (more on that word in a moment) contained per serving. Other high scoring berries that ease soreness are strawberries, raspberries and grapes. Though cherries aren't technically a berry, they also score highly as anti-inflammatories, especially the tart Montmorency cherry which I love to use in my smoothies.

High Antioxidant Foods

"Antioxidant" has been a buzz word in recent years that many of us have possibly become desensitized (another buzz word) to. Antioxidants are the phytonutrients in fruit and vegetables that go after those free radical cells our bodies create as a result of activity, especially exercise. Think of free radicals as something similar to the exhaust created by your car as a result of fuel being burned. When we run, we burn fuel and take in more oxygen which results in oxidation...like metal rusting due to exposure to oxygen. This is why our bodies need foods high in antioxidants.

The following list of foods are **antioxidant** rich and **anti-inflammatory** in nature that you'll most likely see more than once in the recipes to come. It's a good idea to stock up on many of these and have them available for not only the smoothies in this book but also your own future creations:

Fruit
- Blueberries
- Strawberries
- Raspberries
- Grapes (red, black, green)
- Cherries (both sweet & tart)
- Mango (fresh and frozen)
- Papaya

- Pineapple
- Apples
- Lemon
- Lime
- Oranges
- Kiwi
- Avocado (yes it's a fruit)

Raw Nuts
- almonds
- pecans
- hazelnuts
- cashews

Seeds
- flax
- hemp
- chia

Raw Green Leafy Vegetables
- kale (curly, lacinato and purple)
- spinach
- romaine lettuce
- swiss chard
- collards

Other Smoothies For Runners Regulars:

Liquids
- water (of course)
- rice milk
- almond milk
- soy milk
- orange juice
- apple juice

- coconut water (natural hydrator)

Fruit that adds texture & sweetness
- Banana
- Medjool Dates

Sweeteners
- honey (raw or regular)
- agave nectar
- stevia
- pure maple syrup

Spices & Oils
- cinnamon
- nutmeg
- raw cacao powder
- pure vanilla extract
- coconut oil
- natural almond butter
- natural peanut butter
- sea salt

Though it's not always necessary to buy organic, there are some fruits and vegetables that are worth paying the extra money for due to pesticide exposure. The following link has a helpful guide that shows the "dirtiest" and "cleanest" produce regarding pesticides: www.ewg.org/foodnews/summary

Please don't feel overwhelmed as if you need to buy all these things in one trip to the store but I do hope that you're able to give your taste buds the opportunity to try all these healthy foods at some point on the journey. I know I've personally only scratched the surface in terms of food exploration.

It's also similar with running in that we can't put our bodies through all the varieties of training in one session. We continue experimenting by trying new things along the way and eventually forming some positive patterns that yield powerful results.

Top 10 Tips and Tricks for Smoothie Prep

When preparing to mix some of nature's finest ingredients, I've found there are several things that will help make your job easier and more effective. Here are ten tips and tricks that I've learned along the way...

1.) Invest in a Powerful Blender – Though any blender will eventually do the job, not all blenders are created equal. I personally love my *Vita-Mix* (they start at around $350 brand new) which has a 2 horse power motor. This thing can grind a 2x4! *Blendtec* is another powerful brand. If you don't have a powerful blender you'll just need to chop your ingredients a little more. You'll also have to expect smoothies that may have a case of the "chunkies" from time to time (i.e. almond, ice chunks) that may not have blended as well.

2.) Stock Up on Fruit – Keeping your freezer stocked with fruit of all kinds will allow you to have variety in your smoothie choices. Keep an eye open for good deals on fruit in your local supermarket or farm market. For example, I like stocking up on blueberries when they're on sale in season and freezing them. Studies have shown fruit to maintain similar nutrient quality when frozen. Frozen fruit adds a nice thickness to any smoothie. When fresh fruit begins to turn brown (i.e. bananas) simply freeze it and use for smoothies.

3.) Fruity Ice Cubes - Pour fruit juice (i.e. apple, orange, grape, cranberry) into your ice cube trays and freeze them. Make sure it's 100% pure juice with no additives. Coconut water ice cubes are also an excellent way to add nutrients like potassium, magnesium and other electrolytes we runners lose. This will zest up any smoothie in both texture and flavor!

4.) Liquids First - Adding liquids to the blender first will prevent it from binding up on nuts, seeds, powders or frozen fruit and getting stuck.

5.) Ice Last – Adding ice last will insure a smoother texture in your smoothie. Otherwise, you risk a more watery rather than frosty texture if ice has melted significantly before blending.

6.) Start Slow – Always start your blender speed on low before turning up the speed. This will allow time for larger items to chop and eventually blend more evenly. I've made the mistake (more than once) of starting my Vita-Mix on high speed only to see an internal explosion occur where every inch of the container was painted with smoothie.

7.) Smoothie in a Thermos – When you're in a hurry, no worries! A small thermos or insulated travel mug works great to keep your smoothie cool and refreshing on the go. A good thermos will even allow you to drink your smoothie an hour or two later with similar texture and temperature. Simply shake it to remix.

8.) Use Natural Sweeteners – When deciding to use added sweeteners, stay away from refined sugar and artificial sweeteners such as aspartame. Stick with agave nectar, honey, pure maple syrup and stevia. Most of the time I choose to add these natural sweeteners to pre-run fuel smoothies for an extra energy boost or a dessert smoothie where I want that sweeter taste.

9.) Don't Be Afraid to Experiment – There are so many great smoothies yet to be explored! Just as we runners are usually open to experimenting in our training in order to break through to a new PR, we should be open to blending new healthy ingredients for our smoothies. If you think you have a great smoothie recipe, please share it with others.

10.) Buy Organic – Though it's not always necessary and a little more expensive, buying organic ensures that you're consuming the least amount of chemicals in your smoothies. Organic fruit also has richer flavor and more nutrients than fruit that's been sprayed with pesticides or grown in chemically-laden soil.

*Bonus Tip – If you have access to a farmer's market, support your local organic farmers by visiting them regularly for your smoothie ingredients. Outside of having your own garden, this is the best way to buy the freshest fruit & vegetables.

What To Eat Before The Run:
Pre-Run Smoothies to Keep You Fueled

When I was going to college in Anderson, Indiana there was a gas station close to campus where my friends and I would fill up our cars. Not only was this a convenient location, it also had the cheapest gas...*in more ways than one.* This station gained a reputation for having 'watered down' gasoline. No wonder our fuel mileage was suffering, not to mention any possible damage to the engine!

When it comes to powering the human body, there are quality sources of fuel and 'watered down' sources of fuel. From a nutrient standpoint, not all foods are created equal. Gaining some knowledge in this area can mean the difference between feeling full of energy or feeling sluggish and faint as you run- also known as "bonking." I've experienced both and I'll take 'full of energy' any day!

Fuel Systems 101

For the runner, carbohydrates are the fuel of choice due to the quickness in which the body can break them down. The most common carb is glucose. Glucose is like a matchstick that helps you burn fat as well as the only fuel our brains use. It's also what powers our central nervous system. Where's it found naturally? Fruits & honey are the most nutrient dense sources of calories. And it's because of that nutrient density that natural is always better than the man-made, genetically-altered, chemically-loaded substitutes that leave our bodies feeling cheated. Pound for pound, **fruit** is the <u>best</u> source of pure carb energy.

Some delicious examples include…

- Bananas
- Dates
- Oranges
- Pineapple
- Grapes
- Apples
- Strawberries
- Blueberries
- Melon

Not only do these fruits provide the glucose our bodies crave, but they're also great sources of fiber that help bind up the waste that our bodies produce. Studies have shown that most Americans consume an average of 5g of fiber in their diet each day. We're supposed to get 50g. When you consider that a small dish of blueberries provides 15g, it doesn't take a rocket scientist to realize it won't take long to reach that 50g when you're eating the right foods.

Refined = Robbed

Foods that have been refined and processed have been robbed of critical nutrients found only in natural, whole food sources. For example, high fructose corn syrup has been isolated from its whole food source (corn) and placed in countless products that make their way onto our local grocery store shelves (crackers, cookies, soft drinks, sport drinks to name a few). White bread is another example of a food where valuable nutrients have been refined or taken out. Bread made from whole grains is less refined and retains more nutrient value, thus providing a runner's body more of what it truly craves. You may pay less for that loaf of white bread, but you're still being robbed in the end.

As you might imagine, not all calories are created equal. Some are nutrient dense (fruit, whole grains, veggies) and some are just plain empty (or should I say "wimpy"). A few examples of foods full of empty calories include...

- Soft drinks
- Candy bars
- Chips
- Several varieties of snack crackers and cookies
- Many breakfast cereals
- Fruit "drinks" (as opposed to real juice)

Now I'll certainly admit to enjoying a candy bar as a sweet treat from time to time but not to fuel my training runs or races. When we indulge on foods full of empty calories, it's easy to over consume due to their lack of nutrient content. At this point, the body shuts down (that low you feel after the quick high) in order to compensate for the sugar overload. The last thing you want as a runner is a quick high and then...crash! Game over baby.

It's very important to look at the ingredients listed on any item that may catch your interest. There are many products promoting themselves as "healthy" that are anything but. For example, many diet or protein bars are full of refined sugars and high fructose corn syrup. Don't settle for that junk, it's simply a waste of your money.

When Should I Eat Before I Run?

An <u>optimal</u> time to consume your fuel for a training run would be 2 ½ to 3 hours beforehand, but it really depends on the distance you plan on going. Technically, our bodies have enough carb stores to get us through a 1-3 mile run without any problem. Anything longer than 3 miles and it's wise to consume something beforehand. I used the word "optimal" in that first sentence because the body has had adequate time to fully digest and absorb the fuel. In other words, it's available for use. Eating too much without the proper digestion time will many times lead to a pain in your side (aka "side stitch").

Different foods may vary in digestion time. A banana, for example, will digest faster than a piece of whole grain toast. Both are good carb sources but the banana is better when you have less time before your run.

Smoothies As Fuel For the Run

My favorite fuel of choice is a fruit smoothie for the ease of digestion. Food in liquid form gets into the bloodstream more rapidly. Solid food has to be broken down in the stomach before becoming available. A smoothie requires 1 to 2 hours to digest, depending on the size. The following recipes are sure to keep you fueled for that training run or key race on your calendar.

Pre-Run Smoothie Recipes

MEDJOOL DROOL

One sip of this smoothie will have you dancing for joy. Besides their sweet taste, Medjool dates are some of nature's finest energy food that provide quick fuel for the 5k runner or sustained fuel for the marathon or ultra runner. Eating two dates will provide a similar energy effect to eating one gel (i.e GU, Hammer, Clif). A couple advantages with dates are their high iron (blood-building) & fiber (binding waste) content as well as the pure, simple sugars our bodies have access to while running. The coconut water and banana provide a one-two potassium punch that will help ward off those nasty cramps, especially in warm weather. Let the drooling begin!

Ingredients
½ cup rice milk
1 cup coconut water
5 medjool dates, pitted
1 frozen very ripe banana
½ tsp vanilla extract
pinch of sea salt

Directions
Blend all ingredients until smooth & creamy

Nutrition Facts
Nutrition (per serving): 550 calories, 20 calories from fat, 2.3g total fat, 0mg cholesterol, 465.2mg sodium, 1860.2mg potassium, 137.7g carbohydrates, 13.8g fiber, 105.7g sugar, 5.7g protein.

PURPLE HAZE

This recipe will leave you feeling fully alive and give you a healthier high than the kind Jimi Hendrix experienced. Blueberries are the superstar of this show, not only in color but also nutrient value. Consistently ranked near the top of all foods in antioxidant capacity, runners will reap a whole host of cardio benefits including lowering of bad cholesterol, improvement of blood fat balances, protection of blood vessel cell walls and more. The only side effects from this 'little purple pill' are good health. Enjoy this simple rendition of a bestselling hit!

Ingredients
1 cup 100% pure apple juice
1 cup frozen blueberries
1 ripe banana
Juice of ¼ lemon
3 *coconut water ice cubes

Directions
Blend all ingredients until smooth

Recipe Tips
*Coconut water can be found at most grocery stores and is sold by several brands. Pour the coconut water into your ice cube trays and freeze for smoothies.

Nutrition Facts
Nutrition (per serving): 313 calories, 16 calories from fat, 1.9g total fat, 0mg cholesterol, 75.8mg sodium, 921.8mg potassium, 77.1g carbohydrates, 8.5g fiber, 53.3g sugar, 2.7g protein.

HAWAIIAN DREAM TEAM

Sip on this refreshing smoothie an hour and a half before your run and you'll be charged and ready to roll. If you live near the beach, this smoothie is the perfect fit before giving your legs an easy run on the soft sand. For those who don't, a little imagination, a treadmill and an episode of Hawaii Five-0 can take you a long way (about 6-10 miles, depending on your speed). Between the pineapple juice and banana, you're getting a nice dose of potassium & manganese which will help reduce cramping and increase energy production. Aloha!

Ingredients
1 cup pure 100% pineapple juice
1 frozen banana
½ cup fresh papaya, peel & remove seeds
Half of fresh mango, peel removed
2 Tbs dried coconut flakes

Directions
Blend all ingredients until smooth

Nutrition Facts
Nutrition (per serving): 372 calories, 32 calories from fat, 3.9g total fat, 0mg cholesterol, 39.2mg sodium, 1082.1mg potassium, 87g carbohydrates, 7.3g fiber, 62.4g sugar, 3.7g protein.

JUMPSTART JOLT

Looking for that early morning boost before hitting that tempo run or interval workout on the track? This is the smoothie for you. This might also be referred to as "high octane" fuel. A moderate amount of caffeine has been shown to boost performance for runners of all distances, but especially endurance runners. Combined with the coffee, the cacao will add a mocha flavor that many of us are in love with. Add your workout and your eyelids will be wide open most of the day.

Ingredients
½ cup light chocolate soy milk
½ cup strong brewed *coffee or espresso, chilled
1 ripe frozen banana
1 Tbs raw cacao powder

Directions
Blend all ingredients until smooth

Recipe Tips
*Use moderation in coffee consumption. Too much caffeine can cause jitters and create unhealthy cravings. Adjust strength of coffee as desired

Nutrition Facts
Nutrition (per serving): 223 calories, 25 calories from fat, 2.9g total fat, 0mg cholesterol, 91.7mg sodium, 858.2mg potassium, 46g carbohydrates, 7.6g fiber, 23.9g sugar, 6.7g protein.

ACAI ACTIVATOR

Since Acai berries have been known as a "superfood", I guess you could say this is a "super smoothie." When something is referred to as a superfood, it means your body could get nearly all its daily nutritional need from that one food. Nutritionally, acai berries boast the highest antioxidant quantity and contain fatty acids Omega-6 & Omega-9 which help lower cholesterol. Acai has also been called "nature's perfect energy fruit", providing a longer lasting boost than coffee. Ginseng is an herbal root which will provide added energy and increased endurance to this mix.

Ingredients
1 cup *Acai berry juice
½ cup frozen mango chunks
½ cup frozen pineapple chunks
1 Tbs raw honey
½ tsp American **ginseng

Directions
Blend all ingredients until smooth

Recipe Tips
*Most grocery stores now stock their shelves with one or more brands of acai berry juice. Try to select a brand with the least amount of added sweetener.

**Stop by your local health food store to find ginseng, usually in powder or liquid form

Nutrition Facts
Nutrition (per serving): 238 calories, 4 calories from fat, <1g total fat, 0mg cholesterol, 72.4mg sodium, 554.8mg potassium, 59.7g carbohydrates, 2.4g fiber, 55.9g sugar, 1.3g protein.

OATMEAL OCTANE

Some of you may remember those Quaker Oats commercials when Wilford Brimley used to say, "Eat your oatmeal, it's the right thing to do." He was right, of course (I wouldn't argue with him). Oats have a host of benefits including the most popular being the lowering of cholesterol. They're also high in fiber which helps bind up waste and clean the colon. Oats have unique antioxidants called avenanthramides that help prevent free radicals from damaging LDL cholesterol, one of the main causes of cardiovascular disease. Raspberries contain 50% more antioxidant activity than strawberries and also serve to help lower nagging inflammation. This blend is a great fuel choice for that upcoming half-marathon or longer race.

Ingredients
1 cup coconut water
½ cup frozen raspberries
¼ cup plain low fat yogurt or plain *cultured coconut milk yogurt (vegan)
1 frozen ripe banana
½ cup rolled oats
1 Tbs raw honey

Directions
Blend all ingredients until smooth

Recipe Tips
*Cultured coconut milk yogurt is dairy-free and made from coconuts. *"So Delicious"* is one such brand.

Nutrition Facts
Nutrition (per serving): 475 calories, 39 calories from fat, 4.7g total fat, 3.7mg cholesterol, 301.5mg sodium, 1479.5mg

potassium, 101.3g carbohydrates, 15.4g fiber, 53.5g sugar, 12.5g protein.

FIGGY FARTLEK

"Now bring us some figgy pudding, now bring us some figgy pudding, now bring us some figgy pudding and bring it right here..." After singing that line from a popular Christmas carol, did you ever find yourself craving some figgy pudding even though you didn't really know what it was? This smoothie may help satisfy that craving and is sure to make your taste buds sing with its sweet flavor and creamy texture. Figs are a great source of potassium (helps control blood sugar) and among the richest fruits in dietary fiber. Eating figs will also promote bone density with their high amount of calcium, something crucial for a runner's success. Now let's get out the door for that fartlek (Swedish for "speed play") that we're now fueled to run!

Ingredients
1 cup coconut water
2 ripe bananas
4 fresh figs, halved
1 Tbs *agave nectar

Directions
Blend all ingredients until smooth

Recipe Tips
*Agave nectar (also called syrup) comes from the cactus-like agave plant. Sweeter and thinner than honey, you'll enjoy rotating this healthy natural sweetener for your smoothies. It can be found in most grocery or health food stores.

Nutrition Facts
Nutrition (per serving): 399 calories, 13 calories from fat, 1.6g total fat, 0mg cholesterol, 257.5mg sodium, 1672.8mg potassium, 100g carbohydrates, 12.8g fiber, 66.2g sugar, 5.4g protein.

PINEAPPLE PETRO

If you're a fan of Pina Coladas, this is the smoothie for you. You'll be amazed by the energy boost this blend will produce for your next race or training run. Coconut oil contains healthy fats which are ideal for endurance events. I'm also a believer that healthy oils help lubricate runner joints which allows us to feel loose on our run. Speaking of joints, studies have shown limes and lemons to help fight rheumatoid arthritis with their high vitamin C content. I guess you could call it a "joint venture."

Ingredients
1 cup filtered water
Juice of ½ lime
1 cup fresh pineapple chunks
½ ripe banana
½ cup fresh papaya chunks
2 medjool dates, pitted
1 Tbs *coconut oil
4 ice cubes

Directions
Blend all ingredients until smooth

Recipe Tips
*Coconut oil can be purchased at local health food stores or online. One container will last awhile since you don't need to use more than a tablespoon at a time.

Nutrition Facts
Nutrition (per serving): 490 calories, 125 calories from fat, 14.2g total fat, 0mg cholesterol, 18.1mg sodium, 1005mg potassium, 98g carbohydrates, 8g fiber, 81g sugar, 3g protein.

What To Eat After The Run:
Post-Run Smoothies To Aid Recovery

So you've just returned from an intense hour long training run that has you feeling famished. You're hungry so you just grab the first thing in sight right?

Wrong!

What you put into your body after a hard workout or race is just as important as the workout itself. What have you done in the previous hour? You've broken down your body through vigorous exercise. Even during the workout there's a point where the body begins scrambling for rebuilding materials to help repair muscles, tendons, ligaments and bones.

An Observation From the Haiti Earthquake

On January 12, 2010 the world was shocked upon hearing the news of a devastating 7.0 earthquake that killed over 300,000 people and left over a million homeless. My wife Shelley had the opportunity to serve on a medical team nearly a month afterward and she was at a loss for words regarding the damage & devastation around Port Au Prince. Architectural experts have said the loss of life could have been much less if Haiti had stricter building codes in place.

A little over a month later, Chile experienced a much more powerful earthquake measuring 8.8 on the Richter Scale yet the total deaths numbered 521. It's no coincidence that Chile's building codes are much stricter than those in Haiti. One question remains...

How will Haiti rebuild?

That's also an important question for the runner. In other words, what materials will we give the body to work with? The body goes into rebuilding mode immediately. The window of time after a workout to guarantee maximum repair is 15 minutes. It's the most important 15 minutes of your entire workout. It's the time that you ensure recovery from today's run and, in the process, prepare yourself for tomorrow's run. It really can make or break your success...or your body!

An Ingredient For Success

It's very important to replace glycogen stores in the muscles that we lose during the run. Glycogen is what fuels our bodies to function, whether running or just thinking with our brains. The two main sources of glycogen storage in our bodies are the liver and muscles. Our liver can store about 80g which is enough for about 18 minutes of exercise. Our muscles can store 350g which is enough for 70 minutes of exercise.

The "wall" people refer to in a marathon is the point at which those folks have used up stored glycogen. For an elite marathoner, this is around mile 20. For the average runner, this may be in miles 16-18. Whether you're elite or average, when the body uses up the glycogen stores, it's finished. Draining glycogen stores isn't as much of a concern for races or training runs of 10 miles or less. But it's still important to replace what you use during those efforts.

Re-Fueling Suggestions

Our bodies are in a constant state of regeneration right down to the atoms & molecules. This process only speeds up for the runner since we're breaking down our bodies and rebuilding on a daily basis. This is why it's crucial that we refrain from refueling our bodies with artificial, chemically laden food substitutes that our bodies can't process & use. Do you really want your body to be one big molecular candy bar or bag of chips? Whole foods are what the body is craving.

Again, the smoothie is the most efficient way to give the body what it needs after a training run or race. Your body will literally soak up and absorb the nutrients faster in this smooth, liquid form. Why not allow our bodies to have access to key building blocks in the quickest way possible?

Anytime I get a smoothie into my body within that 15 minute window, I feel less soreness, stiffness and general fatigue, even after an intense workout. The following post-run recovery smoothies are sure to give your bodies the advantage they need with quality, nutrient-dense ingredients.

Post-Recovery Smoothie Recipes

CJ's ORIGINAL BLEND

This is the first smoothie I began experimenting with and have enjoyed more times than I can count. Quite simply, this blend contains everything the human body needs in order to recover well. This blend is an antioxidant and anti-inflammatory masterpiece that leaves me feeling recovered and ready for another run within a couple hours. Flax seed is a wonder food that gives our bodies the right kind of fat & protein. A study of forty patients found flax seeds helped lower cholesterol as well as statin drugs...without all the added side effects heard on commercials! Spinach adds green goodness and smooth texture to any smoothie with stealth-like neutral taste.

Ingredients
1 cup rice milk
½ cup pure *pomegranate juice
1 cup raw spinach leaves
½ cup frozen wild blueberries
½ frozen banana
2 Tbs ground flax seed
1 scoop Vega Sport protein powder**

Directions
Place all ingredients in blender and blend until smooth

Recipe Tips
*Make sure to find pomegranate juice with no added sugars. Several brands can be found in most grocery stores

**I prefer Vega Sport Performance Protein which is plant based. Visit www.vegasport.com

If you prefer whey or soy based protein powder, I recommend Hammer products. Visit www.hammernutrition.com

Nutrition Facts
Nutrition (per serving): 665 calories, 126 calories from fat, 14.8g total fat, 0mg cholesterol, 644.3mg sodium, 913.5mg potassium, 112g carbohydrates, 18.7g fiber, 64.2g sugar, 34g protein.

BROC O'BANANA

No matter what your political preference, this smoothie crosses all party lines in terms of post-run nutrition. Broccoli is a cancer-fighting machine and a good source of calcium. There simply isn't enough space here to do justice to all the research done on this cruciferous vegetable. Broccoli combats chronic inflammation, oxidative stress and inadequate detoxification – the three greatest cancer-causing culprits. I can't think of a better time to consume broccoli than after a hard workout when the body is rebuilding and combating free radicals. This hefty smoothie would be a nice follow up to a hard effort of 10 miles or more.

Ingredients
2 cups filtered water
2 ripe bananas
1 cup raw broccoli florets
½ cup frozen blueberries
4 Medjool dates, pitted
2 Tbs ground flax seed

Directions
Place all ingredients in blender and blend until smooth

Nutrition Facts
Nutrition (per serving): 664 calories, 99 calories from fat, 11.8g total fat, 0mg cholesterol, 44.7mg sodium, 1985.5mg potassium, 146g carbohydrates, 21.2g fiber, 99.6g sugar, 11.1g protein.

CHIA CHA CHA CHARGER

Prepare to be fully replenished and recharged after sipping this post-run goodness. Chia seeds have been the craze for the past few years and for good reason. Besides being another great source of omega-3 fatty acids, would you believe chia seeds contain 200% more iron than spinach? How about 500% more protein than kidney beans? More antioxidants than blueberries? No wonder chia seeds are known as a superfood. Many people first heard about chia by reading the popular book Born To Run which also highlighted the Tarahumara tribe of Mexico and their staple use of this powerful little seed. I also enjoy using chia in my pre-run smoothies with their tremendous energy boost.

Ingredients
1 cup coconut water
½ cup filtered water
1 ripe banana
1 cup frozen strawberries
½ cup frozen blueberries
1 scoop Vega Sport protein powder
1 ounce *Chia seeds, grind in coffee grinder for 5 seconds for smoother texture (about 2 Tbsp.)

Directions
Place all ingredients in blender and blend until smooth

Recipe Tips
*Chia seeds can be purchased online or in your local health food & grocery stores under multiple brands.

Nutrition Facts
Nutrition (per serving): 457 calories, 58 calories from fat, 7g total fat, 0mg cholesterol, 784.4mg sodium, 1414.6mg

potassium, 77.7g carbohydrates, 19.8g fiber, 37.3g sugar, 32.5g protein.

AVOCADO AFTERGLOW

As if we're not glowing enough after a satisfying training effort, this smoothie will yield several nutritious benefits including skin health which avocados promote. As for the hemp seeds, the only "high" you'll get is from their high content of rich protein and omega-3 essential fatty acids. They're called "essential" because they're necessary for human health yet our bodies cannot make them on their own. Avocado, flax and hemp are a powerful trio for these fatty acids which are crucial for healthy brain function.

Ingredients
1 cup 100% pure orange juice or fresh juice from 3 oranges
½ avocado, peel & remove seed
1 banana
½ cup plain Greek yogurt or plain *cultured almond milk yogurt (vegan)
2 Tbs organic **hemp seeds
1 Tbs ground flax seed
2 Tbs honey
4 ice cubes

Directions
Place all ingredients in blender and blend until smooth

Recipe Tips
*Cultured almond milk yogurt is dairy-free and can be found in many grocery stores or health food stores.

**Hemp seeds can be purchased in your local health food store or online. I recommend the seeds over powder if you can find them. One popular brand is Nutiva. They're not cheap. Set aside a portion you'll use in the refrigerator and freeze the rest in order to preserve their nutrient value.

Nutrition Facts

Nutrition (per serving): 760 calories, 270 calories from fat, 31.9g total fat, 7.5mg cholesterol, 102.4mg sodium, 1811.8mg potassium, 109.3g carbohydrates, 14.3g fiber, 70.6g sugar, 21.1g protein.

CHERRY BOMB

Cherries and vanilla make a great combination and this blend is no exception. Tart cherries are one of the few food sources of melatonin – an antioxidant that aids in regulating sleep patterns. There continue to be studies that show cherries help decrease exercise-induced muscle damage, something we as runners can benefit from post-run. Enjoy this blend after a morning long run and then enjoy the recovery nap afterward.

Ingredients
1 cup vanilla rice milk
¼ cup tart cherry juice concentrate (no sugar added)
½ cup low fat vanilla yogurt or vanilla cultured coconut milk yogurt (vegan)
½ cup frozen sweet cherries
1 ripe banana
1 tsp pure vanilla extract
1 Tbs ground flax seed

Directions
Place all ingredients in blender and blend until smooth

Nutrition Facts
Nutrition (per serving): 687 calories, 83 calories from fat, 9.7g total fat, 6.1mg cholesterol, 198.6mg sodium, 1473.5mg potassium, 139.4g carbohydrates, 9.1g fiber, 99.6g sugar, 14.1g protein.

GRAPE EXPECTATIONS

You can certainly expect great things with this recovery smoothie. Few fruits have been researched as much as grapes. The fact that grapes are grown on every continent with the exception of Antarctica is reason enough for all the attention. Whether you enjoy a glass of Merlot or down these little guys by the handful, you're getting a host of wonderful runner benefits including decreased inflammation. They are indeed a phytonutrient phenomenon, one of those being resveratrol which has been linked to anti-aging and longevity.

Ingredients
1 cup 100% pure grape juice
½ cup red *grapes
½ cup black *grapes
½ cup green *grapes
Juice of ¼ lemon
3 Tbs hemp seeds
4-5 ice cubes

Directions
Place all ingredients in blender and blend until smooth

Recipe Tips
*Grapes with seeds are perfectly fine to blend into your smoothie. In fact, the nutrition value will be multiplied several times over by doing so since the seeds contain grape oil, the most nutrient dense part of the grape.

Nutrition Facts
Nutrition (per serving): 481 calories, 124 calories from fat, 14.4g total fat, 0mg cholesterol, 27.5mg sodium, 556.1mg potassium, 82.8g carbohydrates, 3.5g fiber, 72.8g sugar, 12.8g protein.

NUTS FOR RECOVERY

You do have to be a little nuts to enjoy this hearty blend. Higher in fat, this smoothie may serve you well on that long run day. Nuts of all kinds are heart healthy with their unsaturated fatty acid content, having a similar effect to olive oil. Contrary to popular belief, nuts actually promote weight loss. In fact, those who eat nuts at least twice a week are much less prone to obesity than those who almost never eat them. This blend will give you more than enough dietary fiber to help bind up any leftover waste created by a workout. Go run then Go nuts...in that order please.

Ingredients
1 cup almond milk or hazelnut milk
½ cup coconut water
10 raw almonds (about a half serving)
10 raw cashews (about a half serving)
5 raw hazelnuts, shelled (about a half serving)
1 frozen ripe banana
2 medjool dates, pitted
1 Tbs natural peanut butter
1 Tbs ground flax seed
pinch of sea salt

Directions
Place all ingredients in blender and blend until smooth

Nutrition Facts
Nutrition (per serving): 652 calories, 282 calories from fat, 33.3g total fat, 0mg cholesterol, 560.8mg sodium, 1484.2mg potassium, 84.2g carbohydrates, 15.5g fiber, 52.8g sugar, 16.5g protein.

STRAWBERRY STRIDES

According to the Runner's World glossary of running terms, a stride is a "short, fast, but controlled run of 50 to 150 meters." For purposes of this smoothie, a stride is a short, fast, but controlled sip of 1-2 seconds followed by pure strawberry ecstasy. Strawberries are a friend of runners with 141% of our daily vitamin C need. As with other dark colored berries, they have a high antioxidant content which helps fight aging and unnecessary inflammation. Basil has been shown to fight unwanted bacteria growth and like strawberries helps decrease inflammation. Remember…short, fast, controlled.

Ingredients
1 cup coconut water
1 ½ cups fresh strawberries
1 frozen ripe banana
½ cup low fat strawberry yogurt or strawberry flavor cultured almond milk (vegan)
¼ cup of your favorite granola
2 leaves of fresh basil
2 ice cubes (optional)

Directions
Place all ingredients in blender and blend until smooth

Nutrition Facts
Nutrition (per serving): 492 calories, 70 calories from fat, 8g total fat, 10.6mg cholesterol, 332.7mg sodium, 1954.1mg potassium, 98.7g carbohydrates, 15.6g fiber, 58.3g sugar, 14.5g protein.

Raw Green Smoothies:
Finding Your Ideal (Racing) Weight

If you've been running long enough, you know there's something to be said about dialing into your ideal weight. Since I began running again in 2008, I've lost over forty pounds which means I weigh what I did my senior year of high school. But it wasn't just the running that allowed me to shed those unnecessary pounds. I had to also begin making different food choices.

When we eat a clean diet, our bodies have a way of falling into a natural rhythm and eventually the weight our bodies were meant to carry. Since we all vary in body shape and size, we'll also vary when it comes to our ideal weight. For me, it's about 162 lbs. Much lighter than that and I begin feeling more lethargic. Much heavier and I feel as though I'm working

39

more than I should on a run. My best racing times have come when I'm near that weight, give or take a pound. I feel strong, full of energy and in proper balance at that ideal weight. How about you? Are you dialed into that ideal racing weight?

If you're currently lighter than you should be, there's a good chance you've been overly concerned about your weight or you're unintentionally not getting the calories your body requires. The best runners are those who know what their ideal weight is and they dial into that weight when racing. For purposes of this section, I'm going to assume that you're carrying a few more pounds than you need to be. Maybe you've attempted to lose weight only to fail.

Incorporating green smoothies into your diet on a regular basis can help shed the unnecessary weight you've been carrying while keeping you in a healthy state. Simply put, a green smoothie has more concentrated nutrition than anything else we can consume. At the same time, it doesn't contain the things that encourage weight gain such as refined sugar, high fructose corn syrup, unhealthy fats, chemical preservatives and other ingredients geared to encourage vicious cravings. It's really the most bang for a runner's buck.

When we run, we not only burn more calories, we're constantly breaking down and building up our bodies. Green smoothies will give us the following added benefits as we seek to build strong, fast, lean bodies...

- It's a quick & easy way to incorporate more greens (Chlorophyll) into your diet

- Boosting of immune system allowing us to run more consistently without getting sick

- Cleanses our organs (liver, pancreas, kidneys, gall bladder)

- It's complete food that's easily digested by our 'running furnace'

- More enzymes which aid in digestion

- More vitamins

- More minerals

- More antioxidants

- Quality protein – green, leafy plants contain the purest form of protein that digests faster since it's high in amino acids (building blocks of protein)

My hope would be for you to enjoy one green smoothie each day, either as a meal or a snack between meals. If you're trying to lose some unnecessary weight, replace your normal breakfast or lunch with one of these green smoothies for two weeks and watch the results.

A Few Valuable Tips For The Best Green Smoothie

By following these basic guidelines you'll make your green smoothie delicious and nutritious...

For green smoothies never blend anything <u>except</u> **fruits, green leafy vegetables, water**

(no vegetables that contain starch, like root vegetables, potatoes, broccoli, beets, cabbage etc.)

<u>Note</u>: tomatoes, cucumbers & avocados are technically fruits.

Keep it **simple** – finding the right combination of ingredients takes a little experimenting. Gradually adding & subtracting ingredients as you get started will be easier on your wallet and your digestive system. Make sure you write down your favorite combinations as a reminder for the future.

Start by blending smoothies that contain **more fruits than vegetables** (about 60% fruits vs. 40% leafy green vegetables) until your palate gets used to the taste of the greens.

Try to **rotate the vegetables** in your green smoothie – For example, use kale on Monday, spinach on Tuesday, swiss chard on Wednesday, romaine lettuce on Thursday, purple kale on Friday. This allows your body to take in a balance of all that nature has to offer.

Use at least one fruit high in **soluble fiber** in order to get a smooth, stable, creamy texture. Fruits rich in soluble fiber include: banana, mango, strawberry, kiwi, pear, papaya, peach, avocado, apple, orange, grapefruit

<u>Note</u>: Fiber in any form helps clean heart arteries, binds up waste and helps remove toxins in the body. It also prolongs the time it takes the stomach to empty so that sugar can be released and absorbed at a gradual pace. Fiber is a good friend of the runner!

The following 8 Green Smoothies have been tried and tested on many a runner's palate.

Raw Green Smoothie Recipes

The following pictures of the green leafy vegetables used for these smoothies may be helpful as you shop for them:

Curly Kale

Lacinato Kale

Purple Kale

Spinach

Swiss Chard

Collards

Romaine Lettuce

KALAMANGO BABY

Sounds like something the Teenage Mutant Ninja Turtles would say. Why do I feel old by even making reference to those guys? I'm pretty sure kale had to be part of their diet with its off-the-charts nutrient density. In its various varieties, kale offers quality protein, cancer-preventive compounds, anti-inflammatory agents, huge amounts of antioxidants and aids the body in flushing toxins. Pears are a great source of copper which will protect against free radicals and also fiber which will keep you regular. Drink up! You know Donatello would.

Ingredients
2 cups of filtered water
1 cup raw curly kale, remove from stalks (about 2 leaves)
1 pear, remove stem
1 banana

1 cup frozen mango chunks
1 medjool date

Directions
Blend all ingredients until completely smooth

Nutrition Facts
Nutrition (per serving): 425 calories, 15 calories from fat, 1.8g total fat, 0mg cholesterol, 48.2mg sodium, 1419.6mg potassium, 108.7g carbohydrates, 15.1g fiber, 73.4g sugar, 6.1g protein.

GREEN POPEYE POWER

Popeye would be proud of this smoothie. We know he gained strength after consuming his spinach, but he was also improving his vision health, bone health and cancer fighting ability. Being able to see well is a helpful quality when we're out on a run. Studies have shown that consuming a mere one cup of spinach per week can decrease age-related macular degeneration (loss of vision) significantly. Unlike Popeye, stick with raw and stay away from the canned version.

Ingredients
2 cups of filtered water
3 cups raw baby spinach
1 banana
1/2 apple, remove stem
6 strawberries, green tops included
1/2 cup cut pineapple
½ cup frozen mangoes

Directions
Blend all ingredients until completely smooth

Nutrition Facts
Nutrition (per serving): 299 calories, 12 calories from fat, 1.4g total fat, 0mg cholesterol, 89.7mg sodium, 1358mg potassium, 74.9g carbohydrates, 9.9g fiber, 53.3g sugar, 5.5g protein.

INSANE ROMAINE

Though lettuce is known to be mostly water, not all lettuces are created equal. Enter romaine. This heart healthy green leaf is an excellent source of folic acid, a B vitamin that combats a blood vessel damaging chemical called homocysteine. Avocado will do wonders to prevent one of the greatest enemies to a runner, unwanted inflammation. It's also a great source of omega-3 fatty acids which helps with blood circulation. You'll also love the texture of a smoothie with avocado.

Ingredients
2 cups of filtered water
1/3 cup young coconut water
2 cups raw romaine lettuce (about 4 leaves)
1/2 avocado
1 apple, stem removed
1 banana
1 cup of cut pineapple
1/2 cup of fresh or frozen blueberries

Directions
Blend all ingredients until completely smooth

Nutrition Facts
Nutrition (per serving): 546 calories, 125 calories from fat, 14.9g total fat, 0mg cholesterol, 119.9mg sodium, 1853.4mg potassium, 109.8g carbohydrates, 19.3g fiber, 75.7g sugar, 6.9g protein.

MULTI-MELON MANIA

This hydration sensation is anything but 'watered down.' Runners will benefit from a variety of nutrients found in these fleshy fruits. The cantaloupe alone will give you 54% of your daily need for Vitamin A. Papaya, called the "fruit of angels" by Christopher Columbus, contains a powerful enzyme called Papain which helps digest proteins. Quicker digestion means our running bodies get valuable nutrients faster and thus our recovery time between workouts is decreased. Melon adds a nice creamy texture in any smoothie!

Ingredients
2 cups of filtered water
1 cup raw curly kale (about 2 leaves)
½ cup cantaloupe melon chunks, skin & seeds removed
½ cup honeydew melon chunks, skin & seeds removed
½ cup watermelon chunks, peel & seeds removed
½ cup papaya chunks, skin & seeds removed

Directions
Blend all ingredients until completely smooth

Nutrition Facts
Nutrition (per serving): 412 calories, 221 calories from fat, 26.4g total fat, 0mg cholesterol, 121.2mg sodium, 1097.1mg potassium, 34.9g carbohydrates, 3.5g fiber, 19g sugar, 18.3g protein.

CITRUS GREEN IMMUNITY

By working this powerful immunity booster into your rotation, you'll enjoy more consistent training that comes from not being sick with cold & flu. Vitamin C also aids in recovery after hard workouts with its healing qualities. Pineapple and its candy sweet flavor contains an enzyme called Bromelain which has been used in treating sports injuries. As runners, may our injuries be few and far between!

Ingredients
2 cups of water
1 cup raw spinach
½ cup raw lacinato kale, remove from stalk (approximately 1 leaf)
1 banana
1 1/2 cups cut pineapple
2 oranges, peeled
½ red grapefruit, peeled
1 tangerine, seeds removed

Directions
Blend all ingredients until completely smooth

Nutrition Facts
Nutrition (per serving): 629 calories, 16 calories from fat, 2g total fat, 0mg cholesterol, 59.2mg sodium, 2194.8mg potassium, 159.5g carbohydrates, 20g fiber, 121.8g sugar, 10g protein.

CHARDONNAYNGO

Doesn't that sound refreshing? Known as the "king of fruit", mangos are renowned for their numerous health benefits including a huge amount of dietary fiber (both soluble & insoluble), Vitamin A (helps vision & skin) and Potassium (regulates heart rate & blood pressure). After removing the peel, feel free to rub the leftover wet underside over your face for a skin moisturizer treatment. With all the exposure to sun & wind, a runner's face can use the extra love. The resveratrol found in the grapes will help keep the walls of our arteries clean. Believe me, when you're kicking to the finish line, you want all the blood flow through those arteries you can muster!

Ingredients
2 cups of filtered water
1 ½ cups swiss chard, stalks removed (approximately 3 leaves)
1 frozen banana
1 ripe mango, peeled
15 green grapes

Directions
Blend all ingredients until completely smooth

Nutrition Facts
Nutrition (per serving): 291 calories, 12 calories from fat, 1.4g total fat, 0mg cholesterol, 134mg sodium, 1122.9mg potassium, 73.6g carbohydrates, 7.9g fiber, 54.9g sugar, 4.5g protein.

GREEN ZING

Looking for something to jolt your taste buds? Look no further than this zinger of a smoothie. If you're a fan of sweet & sour, you'll enjoy this blend. The citric acid of the lime will help burn excess fat for runners interested in shedding a few more pounds. Including the apple seeds is perfectly fine and will give you added cancer cell fighting protection.

Ingredients
2 cups of filtered water
Juice of 1 lime
1 cup purple kale (approximately 2 leaves)
1 granny smith apple, remove stem
1 kiwi, peeled
1 banana

Directions
Blend all ingredients until completely smooth

Nutrition Facts
Nutrition (per serving): 277 calories, 13 calories from fat, 1.6g total fat, 0mg cholesterol, 49.2mg sodium, 1209.7mg potassium, 69.8g carbohydrates, 10.6g fiber, 37.7g sugar, 5.1g protein.

Lean Green Endurance Machine

As a competitive runner, this smoothie is one of my all-time favorites, especially on my long run day. It's the only green smoothie I'm specifically recommending for both pre-run fuel or post-run recovery. If using for pre-run fuel, give this beast 2-3 hours to digest for best results. After experimenting with this magical energy potion in your training, you may find that your body is ready to utilize it as pre-race fuel for distances of half-marathon and longer.

Ingredients
2 cups filtered water
1 cup spinach
1 cup swiss chard
1 cup collards
1 celery stalk with green leaves intact
1 banana
½ avocado
1 peach, pitted
1 pear, remove stem
4 medjool dates, pitted
1 cup fresh or frozen blueberries
2 Tbs raw honey (optional)

Directions
Blend all ingredients until completely smooth

Nutrition Facts
Nutrition (per serving): 820 calories, 129 calories from fat, 15.4g total fat, 0mg cholesterol, 174.4mg sodium, 2724.7mg potassium, 182.5g carbohydrates, 31.1g fiber, 129.9g sugar, 10.8g protein.

Deelish Dessert Smoothie Recipes

Ok, you have a few calories to catch up on and you've got a craving for something sweet. As a runner, you've trained hard and you need a few indulgent rewards from time to time. The following smoothies could also be referred to as healthy 'comfort food.' Whether you've just finished your first marathon or set that new personal best in the 5k, celebrate by allowing your taste buds to run wild with these rich blends.

CHOCOLATE BLISS

This recipe is very simple yet rich in both flavor and nutrition! Cacao has been shown to have more antioxidant flavonoids than blueberries or red wine. Go ahead and sip liberally...your body will thank you.

Ingredients
1 cup rice milk (or almond/hemp/coconut/sunflower seed/soy milk)
1 frozen banana
1 Tbs raw cacao powder
1 dropper *Vanilla Crème Stevia

Directions
Place all ingredients in blender and blend until smooth

Recipe Tips
*Stevia is a natural herb sweetener that's 25-30 times sweeter than sugar and much healthier. For more info, visit www.stevia.com

Nutrition Facts
Nutrition (per serving): 279 calories, 38 calories from fat, 4.2g total fat, 0mg cholesterol, 90.1mg sodium, 422.4mg potassium, 58g carbohydrates, 6.6g fiber, 24.4g sugar, 5g protein.

SWEET N' SOUR LEMON BERRY

When I was growing up, I went a little overboard with Sweet Tarts candy, both the chewy and crunchy varieties. My taste buds still enjoy these flavors but without all the chemicals and artificial colors. This smoothie gives me that fix along with some powerful nutrition. Both blueberries and blackberries rank in the top ten foods containing antioxidants. Studies have also shown lemon mixed with honey can help cleanse the body of harmful bacteria. Pucker up and enjoy!

Ingredients
1 cup coconut milk
½ cup frozen blueberries
½ cup frozen blackberries
¼ cup *coconut cream powder or ¼ cup fresh young Thai
   coconut
½ lemon (remove peel & seeds)
2 medjool dates, pitted and soaked in water to soften
2 Tbs honey

Directions
Place all ingredients in blender and blend until smooth

Recipe Tips
*Coconut cream powder (made from coconut milk) and young Thai coconuts can be found at many health food stores. Search online for the nearest in your area

Nutrition Facts
Nutrition (per serving): 700 calories, 424 calories from fat, 50.7g total fat, 0mg cholesterol, 32mg sodium, 726.2mg potassium, 69.3g carbohydrates, 6g fiber, 49.1g sugar, 5.2g protein.

SWEET N' SALTY NUTTY BUDDY

If you're one of those people who occasionally gets struck by a vicious sweet and salty craving, this blend is for you. Almonds are a fantastic choice for the runner with their high magnesium content which allows veins and arteries to relax and blood to flow more freely. Enjoy this smoothie at the end of a long run day and replace some of that salt you lost through sweat. Don't be surprised if you're accused of being 'nuts.'

Ingredients
1 cup almond milk
½ cup raw almonds
½ cup low fat vanilla frozen yogurt or ½ cup cultured almond milk (vegan)
2 medjool dates, pitted and soaked in water to soften
½ frozen banana
1 tsp pure vanilla extract
½ tsp sea salt
2 ice cubes (optional)

Directions
Place all ingredients in blender and blend until smooth

Nutrition Facts
Nutrition (per serving): 649 calories, 248 calories from fat, 29.1g total fat, 6.1mg cholesterol, 11201.9mg sodium, 1165.3mg potassium, 84.5g carbohydrates, 12.5g fiber, 58.4g sugar, 19.5g protein.

Christmas Noggan' Toboggan (Seasonal)

One ingredient you won't see listed below is holiday cheer, yet you'll find a hefty dose in this seasonal smoothie. I say seasonal since Nog isn't always available year round in some locations. Some benefits found in Nutmeg include fighting cavity-causing bacteria in the mouth, combats asthma, helps relax muscles and has been used for bad breath (your running partner will thank you). Cinnamon is wonderful for runners with its ability to help regulate blood sugar, increase blood flow and relieve arthritis. Researchers say just smelling cinnamon helps boost cognitive function and memory which may come in handy the next time you find yourself lost in that trail race.

Ingredients
1 cup regular egg nog or Silk brand soy nog (vegan)
1/3 cup vanilla rice milk
½ cup low-fat vanilla yogurt or vanilla cultured coconut milk
  (vegan)
½ frozen banana
pinch of *nutmeg
pinch of cinnamon
2 ice cubes (optional)

Directions
Place all ingredients in blender and blend until smooth

Recipe Tips
*Nutmeg should be used in moderation – a pinch or two is considered safe

Nutrition Facts
Nutrition (per serving): 424 calories, 118 calories from fat, 13.3g total fat, 156mg cholesterol, 245.5mg sodium, 911.4mg

potassium, 59.4g carbohydrates, 1.9g fiber, 48.9g sugar, 18.7g protein.

ORANGE DREAMSICLE DELIGHT

If you're a fan of the classic orange creamsicle bars, you'll find your palate enjoying this version with a healthy twist. Most people know that oranges are loaded with vitamin C which helps boost immunity. They're also filled with a phytonutrient called herperidin which lowers blood pressure and inflammation. In order to 'squeeze' the most nutrition out of your orange, leave as much of the white skin found underneath the orange peel. Also, you're much better off drinking a glass of orange juice rather than taking a vitamin C tablet as the body will absorb it much better.

Ingredients
1 cup 100% pure squeezed orange juice
1/3 cup vanilla rice milk
½ cup low fat vanilla frozen yogurt or cultured vanilla coconut milk (vegan)
1 orange (remove peel)
1 tsp vanilla extract

Directions
Place all ingredients in blender and blend until smooth

Nutrition Facts
Nutrition (per serving): 306 calories, 27 calories from fat, 3g total fat, 6.1mg cholesterol, 111.2mg sodium, 942.5mg potassium, 59.8g carbohydrates, <1g fiber, 48.8g sugar, 8.7g protein.

PEANUT BUTTER CHOCO BANANA

If you're a fan of peanut butter cups, not only will your taste buds rejoice, but your heart will too! Peanuts are a great source of monounsaturated fats, the kind emphasized in the heart-healthy Mediterranean diet. In addition, these little legumes contain resveratrol, the phenolic antioxidant found in red grapes and red wine. Finally, a Taiwanese study found that eating peanuts just 2 or more times each week was associated with a 58% lowered risk of colon cancer in women and a 27% lowered risk in men. No need to feel guilty with that extra scoop of peanut butter.

Ingredients
1 cup rice milk (or almond/hemp/coconut/sunflower seed milk)
2 Tbs natural peanut butter
1 frozen banana
2 dates, pitted
1 tsp raw cacao powder
½ tsp stevia

Directions
Place all ingredients in blender and blend until smooth

Nutrition Facts
Nutrition (per serving): 479 calories, 166 calories from fat, 19.7g total fat, 0mg cholesterol, 232.5mg sodium, 740.6mg potassium, 71.4g carbohydrates, 7.5g fiber, 37.9g sugar, 11.7g protein.

VANILLA BREEZE

This smoothie is truly a breath of fresh air. Vanilla has been shown to help reduce anxiety and stress and serve as a calming agent. Women with irregular periods have used vanilla for centuries to help regulate their cycles. Marathon and Ultra runners encountering nausea can find some relief by adding a few drops of vanilla extract to water and sipping it slowly.

Ingredients
1 cup vanilla rice milk or vanilla soy milk
½ cup low fat vanilla frozen yogurt or ½ cup vanilla Rice
   Dream frozen dessert (vegan)
1 medjool date, pitted and soaked in water to soften
¼ cup raw macadamia nuts
1 tsp pure vanilla extract or 1/2 tsp vanilla bean powder
½ tsp stevia

Directions
Place all ingredients in blender and blend until smooth

Nutrition Facts
Nutrition (per serving): 543 calories, 249 calories from fat, 29.5g total fat, 6.1mg cholesterol, 163.1mg sodium, 564.8mg potassium, 63.1g carbohydrates, 4.5g fiber, 44.9g sugar, 10.1g protein.

MAPLE ME CRAZY

I'm a sucker for anything with maple and pecan flavor. I think my brother and I get it honestly from our dad who shared his stash of those little candies known as "nut goodies." I cringe thinking about the days when I would polish off a whole bag in one sitting! No need to feel guilty when sipping on this smoothie. Pecans, as with all nuts, are a healthy way to satisfy a hunger craving. One serving (15 nuts) provides the same amount of protein found in an ounce of meat. A study published in 2004 found pecans (along with walnuts and hazelnuts) contained the highest antioxidant levels of all nuts tested. Maple syrup is a healthy natural sweetener full of manganese which aids enzymes in energy production. It also contains an ample amount of zinc which is needed to help prevent endothelial damage caused by oxidized fats (the endothelium is the inner lining of our blood vessels).

Ingredients
1 cup vanilla rice milk
2 Tbs pure maple syrup
1 ripe frozen banana
½ cup low fat butter pecan frozen yogurt or ½ cup plain
    cultured almond milk (vegan)
½ cup raw pecans
1 tsp pure vanilla extract
½ tsp cinnamon
pinch of nutmeg
pinch of sea salt

Directions
Place all ingredients in blender and blend until smooth

Nutrition Facts
Nutrition (per serving): 826 calories, 369 calories from fat, 43.8g total fat, 6.1mg cholesterol, 167.4mg sodium, 1011.8mg

potassium, 102.9g carbohydrates, 9.1g fiber, 68.3g sugar, 13.4g protein.

Conclusion and Special Bonus

There you have it! 32 smoothies for runners.

And I sincerely hope that you not only enjoyed this book, but also put it to good use by using many of the recipes! If you did enjoy this book, would you post an honest review on Amazon and share about the book with other runners you know?

And the best part?

It doesn't have to end with just these 32 smoothie recipes. In fact, I have several bonuses as my thank you for purchasing this book.

Four Bonuses You'll Get:

The Healthiest Foods: Discover the Top 5 Healthiest Dark Green Vegetables and the Top 7 Healthiest Orange Fruits and Vegetables (PDF report)
Healthy Meal Tracker (PDF)
Weekly Fitness Tracker (PDF)
Healthy Food Choices Affirmation (PDF)

You can sign up for your bonus online here:

www.smoothiesforrunners.com/free-smoothie-recipes

Contact

I'd love to hear from you! Which smoothie recipe is your favorite from this book? What variations worked best for you? *Or just stop by and say "hello!"*

Connect with me at www.facebook.com/runningtipsandadvice. I look forward to hearing from you!

Here's to many great runs ahead,
CJ

CJ Hitz, author of the "*Eat to Run*" series

Who is CJ?

CJ Hitz caught the "running bug" in 2008 and has not looked back since. He's dropped nearly forty pounds in weight, chopped ten minutes off his 5k time (17:40) and has competed in almost 100 races ranging from road 5Ks to trail 50Ks. He absolutely loves running - this most simple of sports - and its many benefits.

He has spent (and continues to spend) hours devouring running magazines, books and websites looking for running tips in all categories. *And now he wants to share these running and nutrition tips with other runners!* Whether you're sitting on the couch contemplating that first 5k or looking to break through to your next personal best, he's excited to help you achieve your goal by sharing the running tips and tricks he's learned along the way. He looks forward to celebrating your achievement. Oh...and he's also a HUGE fan of smoothies!

"Dear friend, I pray that you may enjoy good health and that all may go well with you, even as your soul is getting along well." - 3 John 1:2 (NIV)

Made in the USA
Lexington, KY
23 March 2013